Still Life with Two Dead Peacocks and a Girl

Also by Diane Seuss

It Blows You Hollow
Wolf Lake, White Gown Blown Open
Four-Legged Girl
frank: sonnets

Still Life with Two Dead Peacocks and a Girl

Poems

Diane Seuss

Graywolf Press

This publication is made possible, in part, by the voters of Minnesota through a Minnesota State Arts Board Operating Support grant, thanks to a legislative appropriation from the arts and cultural heritage fund, and a grant from the Wells Fargo Foundation. Significant support has also been provided by Target, the McKnight Foundation, the Lannan Foundation, the Amazon Literary Partnership, and other generous contributions from foundations, corporations, and individuals. To these organizations and individuals we offer our heartfelt thanks.

Published by Graywolf Press
212 Third Avenue North, Suite 485
Minneapolis, Minnesota 55401

All rights reserved.

www.graywolfpress.org

Published in the United States of America

ISBN 978-1-55597-806-8

4 6 8 10 11 9 7 5 3

Library of Congress Control Number: 2017953321

Cover design: Jeenee Lee Design

Cover art: Rembrandt van Rijn, *Still Life with Peacocks*, c. 1639.
        Rijksmuseum, Amsterdam.

To stillness. To life.

Contents

"If a peasant painting smells of bacon, smoke, potato steam—fine."
—Vincent van Gogh

ς

"She is a peacock in everything but beauty."
—Oscar Wilde

ς

"What kind of fuckery is this?"
—Amy Winehouse

I Have Lived My Whole Life in a Painting Called *Paradise*

with the milkweeds splitting at the seams emancipating their seeds
that were once packed in their pods like the wings and hollow bones
of a damp bird held too tightly in a green hand. And the giant jade
moths stuck to the screen door as if glued there. And the gold fields
and stone silos and the fugitive cows known for escaping their borders.

I have lived in a painting called *Paradise*, and even the bad parts
were beautiful. There are fields of needles arranged into flowers,
their sharp ends meeting at the center, and from a distance the fields
full of needle flowers look blue from their silver reflecting the sky,
or white as lilies if the day is overcast, and there in the distance is a meadow

filled with the fluttering skirts of opium poppies. On the hillside
is Moon Cemetery, where the tombstones are hobnailed or prismed
like cut-glass bowls, and some are shaped so precisely like the trunks of trees
that birds build their nests in the crooks of their granite limbs, and some
of the graves are shaped like child-sized tables with stone tablecloths

and tea cups, yes, I have lived in a painting called *Paradise*.
The hollyhocks loom like grandfathers with red pocket watches,
and off in the distance the water is ink and the ships are white paper
with scribblings of poems and musical notations on their sides.
There are rabbits: mink-colored ones and rabbits that are mystics

humped like haystacks, and at Moon Cemetery it's an everyday event
to see the dead rise from their graves, as glittering as they were in life,
to once more pick up the plow or the pen or the axe or the spoon
or the brush or the bowl, for it is a cemetery named after a moon
and moons never stay put. There are bees in the air flying off

to build honeycombs with pollen heavy on their back legs,
and in the air, birds of every ilk, the gray kind that feed from the ground,
and the ones that scream to announce themselves, and the ravens
who feed on the rabbits until their black feathers are edged
in gold, and in the air also are little gods and devils trying out their wings,

some flying, some failing and making a little cream-colored blip
in the sea, yes, all of my life I have lived in a painting called *Paradise*
with its frame of black varnish and gold leaf, and I am told some girls
slide their fingers over the frame and feel the air outside of it,
and some even climb over the edge and plummet into whatever

is beyond it. Some say it is hell, and some say just another, bolder
paradise, and some say a dark wilderness, and some say an unswept
museum or library floor, and some say a long-lost love waits there
wearing bloody riding clothes, returned from war, and some say
freedom, which is a word that tastes strange, like a green plum.

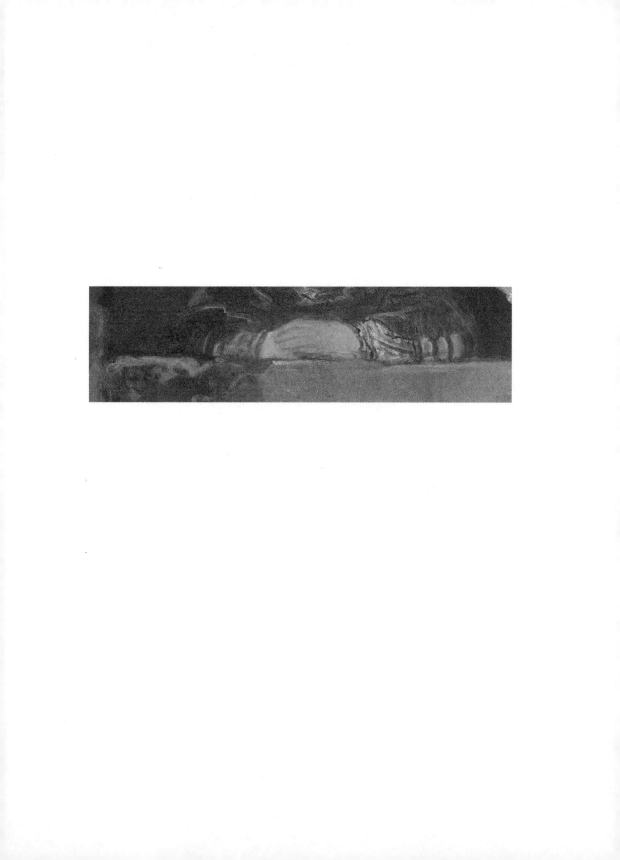

Girl in a Picture Frame

Red velvet she wore, and the rusty casing of a jumper.
Fur collar tight at the throat. A few of the minks
were stripped of their pelts for her, and for her
the gold necklaces and the heavy copper belt

and the ludicrous black hat, big as a tabletop but soft
for her, and the hat band tight around her forehead.
She's too young for earrings, but she's wearing them.
One glints as a band of light moves across the window.

She's fourteen. Her hair is long, and soft and reddish
as a mink. Her eyes unlined and unimpressed, one brow
raised slightly higher than the other. Gaze away;
her gaze will always win. Her interest on the verge

of disinterest, her self-exposure an act of masquerade.
We have painted a frame around her for safe-keeping.
Not barbed wire. Never barbed wire for a girl like her.
If it were wire, she couldn't rest her hands on it

as she does, the right hand half-shadowed but moving
into light, the left already bathed in it, her thumb's
reflection in the high varnish of the little white lie
of the false black frame. Forever on the threshold

of climbing over the edge and displaying something
grand, her spindly naked legs or a deformity of the foot
or nothing at all below the hips, a double-amputee:
she moves around on a cart with bright red wheels.

Memory Fed Me until It Didn't

Then the erotic charge turned off like a light switch.
I think the last fire got peed on in that hotel outside Lansing.
Peed on and sizzled and then a welcome and lasting silence.

Then my eyes got hungry.
They looked at bowls and barn owls and paper clips,
panoramic lavender fields and a single purple spear,

and it was good but not good enough.
My eyes were hungry for paint, like I used to imagine
a horse could taste the green in its mouth

before its lips found the grass.
Then I woke to the words "still life," not as the after-image
of a dream but as the body wakes and knows it needs

mince pie before the mind has come to claim it.
I craved paint like the pregnant body craves pomegranates
or hasenpfeffer or that sauerbraten made with gingersnaps.

Van Gogh ate paint. At least that's the myth of van Gogh.
I ate van Gogh, the still lifes of old boots and thick-tongued
irises. Then my eyes followed the trail back, to Dürer

and his plump rabbit, as perfectly composed as a real one,
as if he'd invented rabbits, and Chardin's dead hare
strung up in a brownish-gold space, its head and ears

flopped onto what appears to be a table, the ears
made of rough bands of white and black and gray
and green-brown paint, the whiskers painted in, the tufts

of fur articulated with white gestures from a thin brush.
And the vanitas paintings of skulls and unspent coins,
and Baugin's dessert wafers shaped like little flutes,

and Pieter Aertsen's *Butcher's Stall with the Flight into Egypt*
in which a small rendering of the Holy Family
is relegated to the background

while the foreground is loaded with gaudy carnage,
a vat of lard, a pig's head hung by the snout, cascades
of sausages, strangled hens, and yawning sides of beef.

The huge gory head of a cow is front and center,
directly below the cool blues of the miniature Virgin Mary
handing out alms to the poor. The cow's cold nose

is so close it makes my eyes water. Its watery eye
gazes back at me and I fall in love. I fall in love again.

Still Life with Self-Portrait

I look at Gijsbrechts' *Still Life with Self-Portrait*,
and I want to touch him. I suppose he was a bad man.
Weren't all men bad back then? Weren't women
bad as well? Or did they only exist within
the confines of the badness of men
and thus come to be known as good? I have
existed within the confines of the badness
of men. Men have existed within the confines
of my own badness. I'm bad enough to admit
I liked it when men existed within my badness
rather than the other way around.

Gijsbrechts appears to be the kind of bad man
who likes to trick the eye. He favored *trompe l'oeil*,
optical illusion. In *The Reverse of a Framed Painting*,
he paints the front of the painting as if
it were the back, complete with wood grain,
framing nails, and a tag—number 36—
seemingly stuck to the canvas with sealing
wax. Aside from this, there is no content.
He has offered you his backside and called it
his frontside, has offered you nothing
and called it something. You've known men
like Cornelius Gijsbrechts.

In *Still Life with Self-Portrait*, he paints
a painting of a painting. It is an unremarkable
still life on what seems to be black velvet.
White grapes with a tendril from the vine
still attached, three peaches, an opened walnut,
and a cut squash. One corner of the velvet
canvas appears to have peeled away from
the frame on which it's mounted, exposing
the wall, the wooden frame, and the stitched
hem along the reverse side of the fabric.
The still life rests on a little shelf he's painted

to mimic a real shelf. It holds his pipe, his
tobacco jar, his brushes, and two pegs
on which hang his gummy palette and a rag.

Alongside the painting of the painting
is a tiny self-portrait that seems to be pinned
to the wall as one would pin a dead moth
to a display board. It is ostensibly the artist
himself, his thick, black hair brushing the top
of his shoulders, his white collar turned down
beneath his paunchy face, his eyes not meeting
mine but gazing off over my left shoulder.
With annoyance? I think he looks annoyed.
Or he's creating the illusion of disinterest.
I've known that kind of man. Or he's thinking,
"This isn't my real face I've painted. She will
never really know me." A man said something
like that to me once: "You don't know anything
about me," a man I'd lived with a long time.
My whole life I've wanted to touch men
like Cornelius Norbertus Gijsbrechts,
but they will not let themselves be touched.

Young Hare

Oh my love, Albrecht Dürer, your hare
is not a spectacle, it is not an exploding hare,
it is not a projection of the young hare
within you, the gentleness in you, or a disassembled hare,
nor a subliminal or concealed hare,
nor is it the imagination as hare

nor the soul as a long-eared, soft-eared hare,
Dürer, you painted this hare,
some say you killed a field hare
and brought it into your studio, or bagged a live hare
and caged it so you could look hard at a wild hare
without it running off into thorn bushes as hares

will do, and you sketched the hare
and laid down a watercolor wash over the hare
and then meticulously painted-in all the browns of hare,
toast brown, tawny, dim, pipe-tobacco brown of hare,
olive, fawn, topaz, bone brown until the hare
became dimensional under your hand, the thick hare

fur, the mottled shag, the nobility of the nose, the hare
toenails, black and sharp and curved, and the dense hare
ears, pod-shaped, articulated, substantial, erect, hare
whiskers and eyebrows, their wiry grace, the ruff of hare
neck fur, the multi-directional fur over the thick hare
haunches, and did I say the dark inside the hare

ears, how I want to follow the darkness of the hare
and stroke the dark within its ears, to feel the hare
ears with my fingers, and the white tuft, the hare
anomaly you painted on its side, and the fleshy hare
cheeks, how I want to squeeze them, and the hare
reticence, how I want to explore it, and the downturned hare

eye, it will not acknowledge or appease, the black-brown hare
eye in which you painted the reflection of a window in the hare
pupil, maybe your studio window, in the hare's
eye, why does that window feel so intimate in the hare's
unreadable eye, why do I press my face to the window to see the hare
as you see it, raising your chin to look and then back to the hare

on the page, the thin hair of your brush and your own hair
waving gold down your back, hair I see as you see the hare.
In the hare's eye you see me there, my swaying black hair.

Still Life with Turkey

The turkey's strung up by one pronged foot,
the cord binding it just below the stiff trinity
of toes, each with its cold bent claw. My eyes

are in love with it as they are in love with all
dead things that cannot escape being looked at.
It is there to be seen if I want to see it, as my

father was there in his black casket and could not
elude our gaze. I was a child so they asked
if I wanted to see him. "Do you want to see him?"

someone asked. Was it my mother? Grandmother?
Some poor woman was stuck with the job.
"He doesn't look like himself," whoever-it-was

added. "They did something strange with his mouth."
As I write this, a large moth flutters against
the window. It presses its fat thorax to the glass.

"No," I said, "I don't want to see him." I don't recall
if I secretly wanted them to open the box for me
but thought that "no" was the correct response,

or if I believed I should want to see him but was
too afraid of what they'd done with his mouth.
I think I assumed that my seeing him would

make things worse for my mother, and she was all
I had. Now I can't get enough of seeing, as if I'm paying
a sort of penance for not seeing then, and so

this turkey, hanged, its small, raw-looking head,
which reminds me of the first fully naked man
I ever saw, when I was a candy striper

at a sort of nursing home, he was a war veteran,
young, burbling crazily, his face and body red
as something scalded. I didn't want to see,

and yet I saw. But the turkey, I am in love with it,
its saggy neck folds, the rippling, variegated
feathers, the crook of its unbound foot,

and the glorious wings, archangelic, spread
as if it could take flight, but down,
downward, into the earth.

Eden: An Outline

I. The question has been can I accommodate this Eden
    A. Without apples or Adam
    B. The only thing slithering, the black sky wriggling free of the stars
    C. The smoke tree
        1. hazy poofs of rusty fuzz
        2. like a circle of unshaved redheads in mid-striptease
    D. Not hyacinths, not hydrangeas
        1. but six-foot-tall stalks covered in unlanguaged vulgarities
        2. put my ear close and hear something like *Fwahhh*
            a. *Fwahhh* darling
        3. the lipsticked center
        4. stamen the color of cream beaten toward butter
    E. Smoke tree sitting back and blowing smoke rings

II. The erotic as Eden
    A. In grade school a kid said the clitoris is a pip or a pearl
    B. He said fuck had to do with a finger
        1. and a Dixie cup
    C. Then I learned that women were flowers
        1. and fucking had to do with pollination
        2. and bee stings
        3. sometimes the stinger gets stuck inside
            a. that'll kill a bitch

III. What if Eden is a storage container for withheld wisdom
    A. Withheld withheld withheld
    B. My grandmother at 92 letting tears rim her little fox eyes about how her husband, after all those ducks and geese and heaving the mess of bluegills on the porch for her to clean, decided to give up hunting
        1. his glass eye finally won the argument about killing it had been having with the good eye
        2. after all those pinfeathers, she said
            a. and let out a long withheld sigh

IV. The white-tailed bird comes close until it decides to be afraid
    A. I see the mechanism of fear
        1. not a gear in the brain but an old decision that digs a grave that erodes into a canyon until nearly everything
            a. falls in
    B. Fear, with its largesse, its spangled silver gown, its icy bracelets
    C. Worry, the little sister in dress-up clothes, believing if she's only alert enough she can detoxify the snake

V. I want no Eden without my mother and sister in it
    A. If my mother and sister live outside the fence
        1. I live outside the fence
    B. My mother climbing the ladder and pulling rotten leaves out of the eaves
    C. My sister using her index finger like a hook to pull the blood clots out of the mouths of the dead
        1. or the impacted turds from the asses of the demented and insane
    D. If I can welcome them in
        1. I will find a way to welcome them in

VI. Like a dog in winter, those inside the gates want out, those outside the gates want in
    A. Did I tell you about my niece who moved to Orlando to get away from the soybean fields
        1. she got a job taking tickets at Disney World
        2. her husband, a pipefitter at SeaWorld
            a. "these days," he said, "it's all about serving the dolphins, the dolphins don't serve you"
        3. in the dead of winter they packed up and moved back home
            a. jerked the girl out of school, she was finally understanding fractions
            b. unpacked the truck
                i. trampoline
                ii. saltwater aquarium
                iii. the dog, Girly, etc.
            c. and started planning a trip to Disney World

VII. The problem with Eden is that it is eternal
    A. It's like that *Twilight Zone* episode
        1. no, not that one, the other one
        2. the one with the train on a circular track

VIII. The problem with Eden is letting yourself have it
    A. Even after you've wrecked it
        1. it comes crawling toward you with its purple mouths
           a. like an army of beaten children
        2. like a ruined dog
           a. it puts its head in your lap and gives you its stillness
        3. it comes buzzing back
           a. like a purple-throated bird with a hypodermic beak
              i. obsessed with your sweetness

Self-Portrait: My Legs

If these legs could talk they'd tell you about Munich.
They'd say "Paris. No one says 'Paris' anymore."
They'd take you on a slow voyage across the channel
from Hoek van Holland to Harwich, drinking all night
with a red-faced East German man who couldn't hear
nor speak. And the British soldier, his narrow
bed and the smell of the pomade in his hair
that marked me for days.

If these legs could talk. All those late-night walks
from E. 7th St. to Sammy Wo's for a whole
steamed fish split between the two of us,
and its eyes, and its lips, and our lips,

and back even further to the summer
I worked as a cocktail waitress on the island.
I was eighteen. Sometimes I'd take the midnight ferry
to the mainland because I could.
I'd sleep in my sleeping bag near the big lake, on the ground.

And the night, as I made the crossing,
it was just me and the hotel magician below deck,
and he offered to hypnotize me for free.
The floor of the ferry was covered in dead luna moths.

That trance he put me in lasted for hours, days.
Maybe he never brought me back, maybe I never woke up
and all of the years since have been an illusion,

as when my right leg shattered like a mirror
and they had to put it back together with titanium
rods and screws. You'll always be in pain,

the doctor said, and yes, my legs would tell you
if they could talk, it's true.

Self-Portrait with the Ashes of My Baby Blanket

Ashes, because she set fire to it in the burn barrel.
Leave her alone, with your newfangledness.
I was a clingy, fearful thumb-sucker, and she knew I needed reinventing.

She tore it away and I screamed and she burned it.
Begone, soft, pale yellow. She knew if I kept it I'd stumble over it
the rest of my life, how far I would travel without it,

and how many strange birds I would trap
in the story of its burning.

Self-Portrait with My Dead Looming behind Me

Mikel, my dad, and Kev, who I nicknamed Bunny
though he buried his softness so deep within

and came across as dangerous, an addict with his knife
and gun and syringe, who once knocked me

across the room for paying back the money he borrowed
from the family with the fat baby who lived on the ground

floor. I've forgiven him. My father, he was perfect
and beautiful, his head tilted like Christ's on the deathbed

pillow, there is nothing to forgive. And Mikel, perfect too,
and so gentle and soft there would have been no irony

in calling him Bunny, so why bother with a nickname?
They fan behind me like the tail of a strange bird,

or like a deck of cards in the hands of a fly-by-night
magician: Pick a card, he says. Any card.

Self-Portrait with Double Helix

Memory returns to me our last encirclement, bones of Mikel's back
beneath my hands. Did I scream all the way to the airport, Alan Martinez,
as you drove with virtuosic madness, and the top down, the old Fiat,

corkscrewed roads leading to the ludicrous interstate and the blue-edged
runway where machines roar as they're forced to defy, again and again,
gravity? In my hands, the book Mikel gave me, my inheritance he said,

Kenneth Patchen. He'd read me a few lines before handing it over:
we shall not be there when death reaches out his sparkling hands
there are so many little dyings that it doesn't matter which of them is death.

The book was used, some of the pages worn through like moth wings
when they've been handled. It's in their DNA to elude handling,
and in our DNA to handle them anyway. You'll forget my voice,

Mikel said, but it coils through me still, like that year we worked
in the bedspring factory, our hands constellated with puncture wounds
from the sharp ends of the copper wire as we fastened spiral after spiral

to cold metal bedframes where someday mattresses would be flung
for cheap deathbeds. After Mikel died, his face lesioned royal purple,
I dreamed a spiral staircase made of the white-blue stuff of stars,

the whole thing spinning at an even pace as if automated, not so much
a staircase as a coiled ladder, and on each rung a soul, miniscule, giving off
a dull glow like a lit cigarette far down the street during a power outage.

Self-Portrait with Levitation

Embodiment has never been my strong suit.
All right, I flew when I was five. Levitated, I guess.
Woke to a sensation of everlastingness, my face
maybe two inches from the ceiling. Floated

there as if in a warm sea. It happened often
until I was ten, when I had the thought
that human beings can't fly and was dropped,
as if from the beak of a large owl, onto the floor.

I was banged up. Cuts and bruises.
From then on, inhabiting my body felt shameful,
like I'd been ejected from the Garden and was
sentenced to a life of peeing and wiping,

hoisting and plugging and unplugging. I'm
thinking that idle travel is a lot like flying,
an enchanting escape from being where you
belong. Some hotel in some city, a bed

swankier than your bed at home, no dead
person's socks flattened at the bottom
of the hamper. As my mother would say
when asked where she went when she took

a ride alone: "I drifted." To belong to the land
and the people that made you is itchy
as hand-knitted wool. Even the word "wool"
made my old friend KK want to pull her eyes

out of their sockets. She told me that
when we were nine or ten. All I had to do
to slay her was to say it: "wool." These things
I know of her: I know she wet her pants

far into her teens. I know that under her clothes
she had eczema. I know her mother dyed
her hair black and wore sweat shields in her
blouses. I know she was Italian, that they ate

spaghetti and meatballs several times a week,
but I was never invited to sit at the table. I know
KK's dad had a vise on a workbench in the garage,
a good tool for opening hickory nuts and squeezing

the heads of Barbies. I know Barbie and Ken
were eunuchs. I know my uncle smoked
while he was on oxygen and that there were fetal
chickens in baby food jars on the windowsill

of his house. I know Freddie cornered my mother
in the garage, Dick made obscene phone calls
to her after she was widowed young, that Bob
Buck peeked in our windows, that some of the boys

in the neighborhood lived alone and raised themselves,
most in grounded travel trailers. Chuck. Leonard.
Rick. Dorian. I know that Bob's Country Club
was really not a country club. It was a bar on a dirt road

with good cheeseburgers and fried mushrooms.
I know the White House was also a bar, on Pucker St.
That my great grandmother farted all the way across
the cemetery as she walked to the outhouse. I know

she read the newspaper upside down. I know her husband
hit a guy over the head with a frozen fish, killing him
instantly, that he went on the lam for years,
sending cash home in envelopes with no return

address, only to discover later on a clandestine trip
home for Christmas that his victim hadn't died at all,
had only been knocked unconscious for a few minutes
and actually woke up an improved version of himself.

I could go on, but you catch my drift. Even when I woke
from sodium pentothal my mother was there waiting for me,
and when I opened my eyes I cried like a premature
baby. There isn't a Holiday Inn Express that can

save me. Not a flight to St. Louis, which my granddad
called Sink Louis, not even a flight to Los Angeles,
where my dad was born and lived next door
to Disney before he was rich and famous, and watched

Walt invent and revise the Mouse in their shared
garage converted into a drawing studio. Where
my dad dropped out of high school and joined
the navy. Boarded the ship that would eventually

kill him. To confess to embodiment is to become
a tender of graves, like my mother, for whom
grave-tending is the only religion. Wash the headstone
like the face of a dirty child, firm but gentle. Deadhead

the bleeding hearts. Everything else is the gilded ballroom
of a grand hotel, live improvisational jazz playing
in the background, birds-of-paradise in tall red vases
on every table, checkout time drawing near.

Still Life with Two Dead Peacocks and a Girl

She comes out of the dark seeking pie, but instead finds two dead peacocks.
One is strung up by its feet. The other lies on its side in a pool
of its own blood. The girl is burdened with curly bangs. A too-small cap.
She wanted pie, not these beautiful birds. Not a small, dusky apple
from a basket of dusky apples. Reach in. Choose a dusky apple.
She sleepwalked to this window, her body led by its hunger for pie.
Instead, this dead beauty, gratuitous. Scalloped green feathers. Gold breast.
Iridescent-eyed plumage, supine on the table. Two gaudy crowns.
She rests her elbows on the stone windowsill. Why not pluck a feather?
Why lean against the gold house of the rich and stare at the bird's dead eye?
The girl must pull the heavy bird into the night and run off with it.
Build a fire on the riverbank. Tear away the beautiful feathers.
Suck scorched, tough, dark meat off of hollow bones. Look at her, ready to reach.
She'd hoped for pie. Meringue beaded gold. Art, useless as tits on a boar.

The Knight's Dream

You dream, like we do, of cash. Cash and clocks and beads. Like us, of masks. Skulls
and masks and treasure and guns. You dream of the curved world. Of ruling it.
Like us, do you wake to an unruly field? Do you stroke, from inside
your trailer, the thoraxes of june bugs pressed against the window screen?
Do you do with your old sadness what the thunderhead does with its rain?
Knight, there's plenty to be sad about. What if you're not really a knight?
What if you're only a knight in your dream? You wake to no glittering
waistcoat and breeches, no black velvet hat, just a shirt and ill-fitting
pants, tight in the crotch or loose in the crotch, from the church donation room.
Nothing to defend but a couple of acres of blighted field corn.
No one feels sorry for you. Too much like feeling sorry for ourselves.
Not even that angel you dreamed up, a long haired boy with barn owl
wings whose missive is, he hallucinated you. You are his fever
dream. The clock's dream, coin's dream. The skull gnaws on the bad idea of you.

Quince, Cabbage, Melon, and Cucumber

Anything can be a marionette. A quince, a cabbage, a melon, a cucumber,
suspended against a black background, illumined by a curious
white light. In this little show, the quince plays a full gold moon. The cabbage
is the antagonist, curled outer leaves fingering the charcoal void.
Cucumber's the peasant, nubby belly to the ground like a frog.
That leaves melon, center stage, rough wedge hacked out of her buttery side.
Each object holds its space, drawing the eye from quince to cabbage, melon
to cucumber, in a left to right, downward-sloping curve. Four bodies
hang in the box of darkness like planets, each in its private orbit.
It's a quiet drama about nothing at all. No touch, no brushing
up against each other, no oxygen, no rot, so that each shape, each
character, is pure, clean in its loyalty to its own fierce standard.
Even the wounded melon exudes serenity. Somewhere, juice runs
down a hairy chin, but that is well beyond the border of the box.

The Last Still Life: The Head of Medusa

There are stories we refuse to tell. To tell them would be to set them
loose upon the world. Like the girl (not innocent, no one's innocent)
whose body was swooped down upon by a larger, meaner, murkier
story like an enormous granite pestle that crushed her own winsome,
soft, unconscious, run-of-the-mill story into something like cornmeal
mush. Then once upon a time (there is no once, there is no time) the girl
was winnowed down like a bar of soap. She cut off her hair and refused
to wash it. Beauty's so dumb, she was known to say, isn't beauty dumb?
She moved into a rusted-out potato-chip delivery van
between the gasoline storage tanks and the river. She kept a clump
of snakes in a green steamer trunk. Black ones. Gold, with patterns. Real writhers.
Once she became a full-fledged woman, things around town started turning
to stone. The dam dried up. Fields, banks, and meadows. No rain. Then, overnight,
the burial ground became a parking lot. All was stillness. The End.

Walmart Parking Lot

Jackson Pollock

Frozen Coke splatter, and the disembodied sadness of the one who accidentally dropped it. Vomit-arc. Winding loops of coal tar sealant. Sparrows, too, have left their mark. From above, a seagull has mistaken it for a large body of water and glides on air currents, screeching intermittently, looking down, as if on holiday. The rectangle has no interest in telling you a story. Its debauched energies hum like telephone wires after the last caller has been taken off of oxygen.

Mark Rothko

Some of us would take the South Shore to Chicago to see art. We'd stand in front of large canvases in palatial museums, speaking to each other in invented languages. We wore solid yellow shirts and red pants, with a rope belt demarcating the blocks of color, befuddling the critics. The art, we saw, was good. We swallowed it down hungrily, without filter, like drinking water straight from the creek, no matter the risk, because it tasted so sweet. We rode the swaying train home at sunset, the smokestacks of Gary shooting flames into a sky already clanging orange. The city had been a dream. Home, too, a dream, black above, silver-gray below, floodlit by buzzing security lights.

Georgia O'Keeffe

From above, we'd like to believe, it's made of the same bone that we are. How high would we have to go to see it as the skull of the deer we found summers ago in the creek bed? Deep down, we know it was not born and cannot die. Or it is death, the everlasting kind, not like a field, not at all like a field, which lives even as it dies, and dies as it lives. Also unlike the field, there was a time before this was here. It moved in, but we don't remember when, like a stepmother who came so long ago she's erased all memory of our mother.

Andy Warhol

To enter the store is to be seen wanting. We have deposited our checks. Now we buy the CD of the girl who sounds like a naughty baby. Now we buy the skirt, the top that shows our belly, and the Dexatrim that will shrink it so it can be shown. We buy a self-frosting kit for the spikes of our hair and the gloss that frosts our lips with cold dew. We are saving up for a barbwire tattoo. The nose piercing went wrong. We hemorrhaged for days, had to remove the stud and let it heal over, leaving behind a weird scar. Don't show us as we are, walking to the car in the heat that radiates up from the cement they laid over the burial ground. Show us only when we're ready, and when we're ready, show us large, but to get ready will take us years.

Alice Neel

Like you, our nostrils are asymmetrical. Like you, our ankles swell. Our children, in their specificity, look like monsters. You must confront our terrible nakedness, our nipples swollen and dark, our bellies marked with the dusky purple latitudinal line of pregnancy. Our pubic bushes are thick and red, or black and spare, or we are old and left alone with a gray thatch. If we are children, we're bare and unashamed, our hands on our hips, until we are shamed. Like you, we enter the store. Like you, we exit. The light outside will not relent.

American Still Lifes (the Gothic Sublime in 102 Syllables)

Still life with stack of bills phone cord cig butt and freezer-burned Dreamsicle

Still life with Easter Bunny twenty caged minks and rusty meat grinder

Still life with whiskey wooden leg two potpies and a dead parakeet

Still life with pork rinds pickled peppers and the Book of Revelation

Still life with feeding tube oxygen half-eaten raspberry Zinger

Still life with convenience store pecking order shotgun blast to the face

Sentences

Sis moved back and forth from Cheetos to M&M's.
Lil talked a blue streak, sucking from her baby bottle between sentences.
Little Ro showed up without pants or a diaper.
What's that dick smell, Sis asked.
That's when the goat showed up.
The Jesus camp kids walked back to their own yard, single file.

Hold your horses, Lou said that night to her dead sister, wait up, I'm on my way.
She used her last trip out of the house to make her own arrangements.
When she opened her purse to get out the cash to pay them, it smelled like a purse.
I want my own pillow in there, and the blanket with the bees on it.
Let me wear this hat, she said, trying it on so they'd remember.
She looked at them hard through the veil.

Betty got to where she couldn't live in a house anymore.
She took a Singer dress form off its tripod, cut it open and used it as a suitcase.
She had a carrot peeler in there, bar of soap wrapped in wax paper.
Buffalo head nickels and some bones, but she never said whose bones.
She wore a round, hollow one on her finger like a wedding ring.
She toted that thing around town like a kid too old to be carried.

May was just a skeleton with a few blue-white hairs stuck to the skull.
She'd been like that for days, on the couch with the TV blaring.
The whites of her eyes were the color of egg yolks.
May wouldn't blink, afraid her eyes wouldn't open again once she shut them.
Her lungs fluttered like two pink pillowcases on a clothesline in a stiff breeze.
She had one of those smiles on her face like she was getting away with something.

Chris said, tell me you're not fighting over a McNugget, you two.
Little Ro's big ears made him look dumb, but he wasn't dumb.
He took out his measuring tape and measured a french fry.
Chris had given up on lipstick but she still used the blush with gold sparkles.
No ball pit until you finish your Hi-C, she said to all three of them.
Little Ro peed his big-boy pants while measuring the cash machine.

They all got pink eye and then strep and then double ear infections.
You're all going to need tubes in your ears, the doctor said.
Chris laid in a supply of popsicles.
Brian was doing ok until he shot his gun in the air for fun and broke his eardrum.
The rooster went after Sis, so Brian put it in a sack and hit it a few times against a fieldstone.
Three sick kids and a sick man and her own ears so plugged up she couldn't hear the baby.

They took away Jim's gun, but if he decided not to put up with it anymore he'd find a way.
He sat there smoking weed and washing down pain pills with a 40 of Olde English.
Try to imagine what it's like without legs, he said.
Back in the day, his wife said, how many times you going to say back in the day?
If I could walk, I'd pop her one, he said, and blew out a long stream of smoke.
I'll tell you what, Jim said, back in the day, I would have been dead a long time ago.

Hindenburg

And I'm like he's got a tumor the size of the Hindenburg and she's like in his belly and I'm like no not in his belly hell the belly would be a blessing the belly would be all John 3:16 and then I'm like no it's in his neck it's in his goddamned neck and I blame the government and she's like who do you blame and I'm all I blame the government and she's like if I were you I'd blame the bug spray you remember how when we was all kids how the little yellow airplane would bug spray the soybean fields and I'm like oh you better believe I remember but with him the bug spray was small potatoes compared to Nam and she's like compared to what and I'm like compared to Nam to Vietnam and she's like oh Vietnam he was over there for how long and I'm like long enough I'm all long enough to end up with a tumor on his neck the size of the Hindenburg and she's like the size of what and I'm like the Hindenburg and she's like what's the Hindenburg and I'm all it was a balloon a balloon that caught fire in the sky and she's like a balloon on fire and I'm all a balloon on fire and she's like a balloon doesn't seem that big and I'm like that one was

There's Some I Just Won't Let Die

I don't care how many times they reach
out to their dead sister reach away I say
you're not dying even if all that's left of
them is a skull with one long silver hair
sticking out of it some even all the way
dead and I'm like a schoolmarm pulling a
kid back into the classroom by the hem of
her dress when she climbs out the window
to run home to mama it's like I'm saying
you sit in that chair and learn your times
tables little miss back then a teacher could
slap a kid when they needed to be slapped
hard enough to leave a handprint oh no
you don't I say and I hook my finger
inside their mouth and pull out a clot like
a blood plum the kind pops used to make
into cordial but pops is gone and with
him the recipe and the mystery of how he
managed to get a bushel of blood plums
in the middle of winter

Bowl

We work at the factory until it shuts down and then we work in the deli section or the meat counter. If a girl gets pregnant we throw her a baby shower with ice-cream cake if we're all chipping in. No matter if it's the second marriage or the third we hire a party bus and all us girls go out on the town, barbeque, bowling, and a Black Sabbath tribute band. If, in the photos, our faces look haggard or sad, it's because you caught us at a bad moment. We are not haggard or sad. When the baby is born we'll ringlet her hair. If it's a boy we'll cover him with socket wrenches and fire trucks. If the siren makes him scream we will distract him with a tit until he's too old for tit and then we'll distract him with a slice of ham and some American cheese. We do not want to be strange with one horn growing out of our foreheads. We want to be what the others have been, sit on the same stool the others have sat on when our ankles swell. All of our ankles swell. We are usual. We are like bowls. There have always been bowls. They're shaped the way they are for a reason. Yes some have curlicues or paintings of angels but a bowl is a bowl and it has always been a bowl and it was here before you came and it will outlast you.

American Run-On Sentences

HOG MARKET

bring your full-grown hogs to the white cinderblock free mermaid tails out front

OVERSIZE LOAD

you'd think they wouldn't crowd the center line hauling carnival shit fools

JESUS IS REAL CAMPGROUND

got stocked fish pond free baptisms check out the view from calvary hill

CORN MAZE

we grew it screwy like to see people pay to get lost real crows too

DEER PROCESSING

the point of this business is to use every part testicles

I Look at My Face in a Red Mylar Balloon Tied to a Mailbox

Behind me the remains of the cinderblock tabernacle
and behind me the west-leaning house with a red dirt floor

and a stop sign on fire
and a horse galloping past with red foam on its lips

and Rhonda with the rusty birthmark on her neck who could lasso anything
and Rick playing the blues in his red trailer with his waist-length hair
and Ellie pregnant with his baby, her red belly button turned inside out

my beet-colored hair blown over my eyes
my mouth, bloody as if recently beaten

and when the wind blows the balloon closer, all I am is wounded mouth

when I open it, I can swallow the town

Stateline Pastoral

Our hair is large. It contains multitudes
of pins and nits and bows. Our bodies are wrong but coherent.

Love is our mission,
the wedding, our modus operandi, our peep show and opera.
Once it's over, our beauty's spent.

The fiancée is not so much human as integer.
If the wedding's in winter, with fur
sewed to the cuffs of all formalwear,
by spring the corset bones are exposed.

June's the unlucky month.
All the county's porcupines are intent
on puncturing the dream.

When the freezer shuts down, we lose
the side of beef, top of the cake, and the bouquet.
For a minute there, everything looks
freshly killed or baked or picked.
We're dizzied by the raw scent of tea roses.

Autumn's when the bruises show.
Kicked by a horse, we've said for generations.
Same horse, dumb, unsaddled, glass-eyed, white,
with fire flaring from the nostrils.

Weirdly, when our noses are broken and our houses
foreclosed, that's when things get good.

We die on our Harleys, driving too fast on unnamed roads.
Our bodies fly backward, nostalgic
for a past that never happened.

Our souls stay with the bike, moving
forward through cattails and daylilies.

We're leery of books, the way they colonize
the imagination, and films, which infiltrate dreams,
though at times we'll flock to movies with explosions,
for explosions clean out the carburetors of ourselves,
unless we're pregnant, for movie explosions
have been known to cause miscarriages.
Those of us haunted by war
will sometimes turn to books to combat nightmares,
choosing, from the shelves of the old library,
the weightiest, the ones with a thousand pages,
as if the object of the book, held close, could replace
a dead comrade, and maybe it can, at least for the hours
and days it takes to mouth each word like a newborn
pig mouths the line of tits on its mother's belly.

There's that man again, a former soldier,
and once a soldier always a soldier, the one

with the terrible limp who slurs his words
into a new language, grotesque,

though we nod and furrow our brows in understanding,
for we do understand the intention beneath the words.

He's reading *War and Peace* again, but this time
from back to front, and so he refers to it, in his mind,

as *Peace and War*. We can tell by his wry smile.
He's known for his wry smile.

The rest of us prefer what lies below what is called art,
the source of art, the raw field and not the story of the field,

and love, even when it's guttural,
especially when it's guttural and married to suffering,

which we trust.
We're told to read the Bible but the Bible is another book,

and halfway through Genesis we feel as if we're back in school,
stuffed into our desks watching some teacher

murmur on endlessly about things that happened
far away from here,

when all we want is to be home wearing our muddy field boots,
sitting on an upended bucket, shelling peas.

We wear our hairdos long and tumbled back like vine pours weighty
down a chain-link fence. We go, at times, unwashed to craft
that warm, green stink of algae-covered inland pond and grass-fed
cud. With the contents of one box and one can, we bake something
so sweet and gold you'll want to marry the pan. In this way,
we are alchemical. If it's pretty, we taxidermy our kill.
Here, a bear bigger than a travel trailer. There, an unnested baby
swallow small enough for the apex of a teacake. When asked
directions, we reference the red chickens, though they scatter. Turn

right at the red chickens or left, or if you see the red chickens you've
gone too far. We believe in the mortuary sciences and chip in
to charmingly lay out our dead in yellow silk as if they were rich
and cunning. At viewings, we talk about their mouths, how any moment
a word could come spilling out. Our decisions are poor, our work ethic
unfledged, our children are cockleburs in the far field, their branches,
terminal. In our midst, a woman who dances until her pudendum
is raw, which she announces from the top of the empty water tower.

Our memories are local, acute, and unrelenting.
Our hope is to quash them. Fields invite them,
and fog. So out of the brume that rises up
from snow in the spent vineyards comes a man

back from war, singing as he used to sing, such
large notes out of a small, skeptical mouth. Later,
his liver swells up like he is with child. And drifting
out of the burned field, that couple who lived

by the train tracks, their house smelling of pitch
from the wooden ties, and of mutt, from the lineup
of terriers they used in their trained dog act,
which they displayed in shabby, off-brand

traveling circuses throughout the Midwest. Once
even Texas. Harry and Jessie. Some of us never
laid eyes on them, and still we're saddled with them.
Saddled, as if we're the horse and memory the heavy

rider. We remember the hound whose smooth, warm
head we never stroked, whose relentless howling
was quashed by a can of pork and beans thrown
from an upstairs window, who keeled over dead

and was buried by the gravedigger, as a favor,
to pay a debt about which the less is said the better,
Dan, the hound, who resurrected the next morning,
used his fat paws and thick, black toenails to dig

his way out of his own grave, whose sad bay persisted
for years, long past his actual death, and still persists.
It has become a burdensome song we hum
sometimes while nursing the sick or doing dishes.

The Hand Has Dropped the Fruit and It's Painted Where It Falls

or such is the theater of painting for every painting is a performance some complete with curtains pulled away for the spectator to see the fruit as if casually dropped and painted where it falls or the hare strung up or the turkey hanged from one gnarly foot as if the painter had no design on reality but only painted it haphazardly an improvisation of objects in space but actually a performance of haphazardness as if to say art is not artifice it meets you where you shrug off your robe or pile your strawberries in a basket with no eye for composition but even the haphazard is arranged by the eye was it Rimbaud who said a derangement of arrangements

thus Williams's so much depends upon a red wheel barrow glazed with rain water beside the white chickens is anything but an accidental tableau viewed for instance through a window as he tended a dying woman in her bed one hears the rhymes of glazed and rain and barrow of wheel and water and white of depends and chickens and considers how briefly water glazes a surface before it must evaporate and leave us behind and how quickly chickens flap their filthy wings and scatter how wheel is separated from barrow rain from water white from chickens so that all constituent parts of what appear to be simple solid randomly arranged objects have been factored down to their prime numbers how nothing is casual nothing is uncomposed whether a curtain is drawn away from the deathbedroom window or not

I Look Up from My Book and Out at the World through Reading Glasses

The world, italicized.

Douglas fir blurs into archetype,
a black vertical with smeared green arms.
The load of pinecones at the top,
a brown smudge which could be anything: a wreath
of moths, a rabbit strung up
like a flag.

All trees are trees.
Death to modifiers.

A smear of blue, a smear of gold that could be a haystack,
a Cadillac, or a Medal of Honor without a neck to hang upon.

I know the dog killed something today, but it's lost in fog.
A small red splotch in a band of monochromatic green.
And now, the mountain of bones is only a mountain capped in snow.

It's a paradise of vagaries.
No heartache.
Just an eraser smudge,
smoke-gray.

All forms, the man wrote, *tend toward blur*.

Silence Is So Accurate, Rothko Wrote

Accurate like an arrow without a target
and no target in mind.

Silence has its own roar, or not-roar,
just as Rothko wrote "I don't express myself
in my paintings. I express my not-self."

A poem that expresses the not-self.
Everything but the self.
The meadow's veil of fog, but is veil self-referential?

Already, dawn, the not-birds alert to what silence has to offer.

The fog, one of Rothko's shapes,
hanging there in the not-self, humming.

Mikel, before he died, loved Rothko most.
When he could still think, he put his mind
to those sorts of judgments.

If I pull the fog away like theater curtains, what then?

Sadness shapes the landscape.
The arrow of myself thwacks the nearest tree.
Fog steps closer like a perpetrator or a god.

Oh. I'm weeping.
Tears feed the silence like a mother drops
into her baby not-bird's open beak

some sweet but dangerous morsel.

It Seems at Times That Silence

has a roundness like an apple,
and that even an apple is made
of planes, minute horizontals
and verticals, ruby and russet
and freckled and spackled
and black. And that silence
is really not bereft of sound,
it's only that a heavy stratum
of noise has been lifted up
to expose the resonances
below: eccentric cries of birds
which might be called lonely,
and the workaday discourse
of insects, and the whistling
of something rising up
or falling from the air.
If this layer could be lifted
like a cool, flat rock at the base
of a fir tree baring the writhers
beneath, and the layer of minuscule
sound below, and the layer below
that, the final silence might be
found, the last one, turning
round on its stem like an apple.

Still Life with Dictator

Anyone can look at a bowl filled with plums.
Even the ones trampled beneath the hooves
of the general's white horse—the peons,

the threshers, the nobodies. Food, the great
leveler. The nobodies must eat, even if
they resort to coffee grounds,

or sandwiches airlifted and dropped
into the jungle, teeming with maggots.
Food is food. Even the general must eat.

Even presidents, dictators. Hitler himself
would walk along the cliff's edge from his
compound in Berchtesgaden to the round

teahouse in the trees. He'd settle himself
into the cushioned chair some nobody pulled
out for him, and into the nose, positioned

over that cowcatcher mustache, came
the scintillating fragrance of tea roses.
"There must be fresh flowers!" he'd barked

at the peons. As the steam from his tea
dampened his mustache, his eyes lit
on the white bowl aloofly holding

ten plums. He wanted to upend them, send
the white bowl spinning until it hit the curved
wall and broke into baby teeth.

"Who cares?" he wanted to say to the plums,
but they wouldn't listen. Such an ordinary fruit;
he'd seen the nobodies wolfing them down

and spitting the pits in the air. Braying like donkeys,
like schoolboys. The plums mocked him
with their stillness. The sugar bowl mocked him,

the sugar spoon engraved with the fat head
of a thistle. Fruit sickened him, with its worms
and scars, its fermentation. Its plainness,

its roundness, its calm. It stared at him
like one of those nobodies who didn't care
how many times it was whipped. One

of those who claimed to be beyond pain,
one with a glint of what the churches
would call holy light in their eyes. Plums,

taunting him until he grabbed one
and bit down and let the gold flesh
fill his mouth with its revolting sweetness.

The Heroic Penetrates the Quotidian

but the quotidian, like a cockroach,
has strength in numbers. The general
rears up on his steed, the angel

fills the canvas with her astonishing
illuminations, while the quotidian plods
on, dull-eyed, or doesn't plod at all.

It's a knife, a spoon, a wooden chair,
a pan, a log wrapped in blue flame.
The general has his sword and his story,

the angel her voluminous wings and her
song, but the quotidian's only weapon
is stillness. Yet, everything caves to it.

Look at the general, he's nothing
but bones in a moth-eaten uniform,
the angel, an adornment on his tombstone.

His story is snapped up by the tongue
of a frog. Her song is crushed
under a bowl of apples.

Silence Again

My mother had been sitting at his bedside for years.
Her exhaustion, epic. "Go home," her friend ordered.

"I'll sit with him. Sleep." This was Jan, who lived
and died in her parents' fieldstone house, and liked

to sleep with the windows open, even in winter,
to let the snow heap on her bed. He died while

my mother was absent. They do that, the dying,
waiting for someone to arrive or depart. Jan was

enough of a friend to sit there until the heart monitor
went flat, to shut down his eyes. She, too, died young,

a decade later, in a hospital bed in her parents' house,
her head bald from chemo. I picture her down

on her knees in late spring, mudding-in the flowers.
That's what she called it, mudding them in.

My father, after all the yelling when he was a boy,
the threats, the bottles of whiskey, the guns,

and the racket of war when he was on that ship,
the *Nashville*, finally got to open up his arms

to silence. Now, when I embrace it, silence,
especially at night, in the dark, I see my father's

name, as if silence were a canvas he painted,
and his signature there in the corner.

Memento Mori

All my life, I've been writing of it but not from it, directing
a bare lightbulb at its profile so I may outline its silhouette

on tracing paper. Its gifts have been delivered to my door
in an unattributable basket, food nameless but nourishing,

the cook, anonymous, the recipe, untranscribed. I saw
my father carried from the couch into the waiting ambulance,

which wailed like my mother could not, like I did not,
as wailing is an art, its permissions, learned. The rotating

emergency light swept across his face like a rash, a red tide.
I was not there when he died. I was at school, learning

equations, trying not to pee my pants because peeing them
meant getting my wet bottom slapped by the teacher

and carrying the soaked underpants home in a paper bag.
Even if I'd been there, if I'd touched his face

with my fingers dirty from recess, I'd know nothing more
of it than I do now. He was so young, and death froze him

in time. If I knew him now I'd be his elder. I could tell him
to pick up after himself. To shut the door against the heat

or cold. His illness made me conscious of the veins beneath
the skin, the blue of a bruise and its gold aura, the bones that rise

through the skin when one has been sick for a long time, unable
to wear a suit and tie anymore, wrapped only in a blue robe

belted at the waist, and a back brace. He'd take short walks
up and down the sidewalk in front of our house, pacing,

my mother called it, a word I contemplated, as I did the word
"throb," until they became part of my consciousness, just as I imagine

he contemplated the thing inside him, the thing he was inside,
or soon to be, like a man walking the gangplank contemplates

the sublime blackness of the sea. Once, I ran from the school bus
and leaped into his arms as he paced, like a girl in a movie. Knocked

his chin with my skull, made him bite his tongue. He stuck it out
to show me the blood my performance had cost him. Blood type

O negative, which later I'd seek in other men, his disease,
histiocytosis X, which together made tic-tac-toe. We played it

sometimes in the hospital room, but our hearts weren't in it.
Is anyone's heart in tic-tac-toe? It's a game built for hospital rooms.

His abdomen was interestingly swollen. His hands strangely cold.
My face oddly ugly as I cried looking into a hand mirror.

My consciousness growing adverbs, distended with them.
The transformation was incremental; he'd been sick

my whole life, six years, then seven, so what I knew of Father
was a body in constant progression, though toward what end

I could not imagine. The closest I can come to empathy for that
destination is when I was put under for surgery. Ten, nine, eight,

gone. No comfort, no embrace, only absent, an empty desk at school,
an empty coat hook, a locker resonant with its own hollowness.

On the day he died, I walked alone up Fulkerson Rd. to my
Brownies meeting, pressed my forehead to the screen door before

opening it and heard the girls inside praying for me. Absent
but present. Present to my absence. Is this death? For a while, I thought

it belonged only to my father and family pets. It was months before
I understood my mother too would someday die, any time she left

the house she could die, like when she went on a three-day bender
with her brother and was spotted all over town, flipping burgers

at the Four Square, laughing or crying and dancing at the cemetery,
and I lay awake at my grandmother's house, in the bat-filled dark,

waiting for word of my mother's demise, drunk and hit by a train
at the unmarked railroad crossing by the underground house.

Even at home, watching *Shock Theater* on TV, pounding meat
with a mallet, reading a book, the one titled *How to Raise Children*

at Home in Your Spare Time, death could take her. Only later, after
shooting a rabbit in mid-leap, I saw that I could kill and I, too, would die,

that my father beckoned me like Ahab in Bradbury's adaptation
of *Moby-Dick* for film, his body lashed to the whale by ropes,

his dead arm flagging back and forth with the heaving sea, mindlessly
beckoning, for the dead are beyond caring whether we follow them

into the brine or not. My father's journey was one of disconnection
and reconnection. His mind carried him back to the ship he boarded

at seventeen, escorting MacArthur back to the Philippines.
In his delirium he shouted for the General, he was a sailor in his dying,

an archetype, not a family man. Have you traveled, in your wanderings,
to the Chapel of Bones in Portugal, the walls lined with human skulls,

femurs, fibulae, and teeth? Over the doorway: "We bones that here are,
for yours await" troubled me, its syntax unclear. Its arrangements

and sequencing. I tried to link one word to another, like struggling
to turn a bunch of reclusive birds, each the only one of its species,

into a flock. "We bones," as if the bones are sentient beings,
like greeters at Walmart who are there to remind us that we, too,

will be greeters at Walmart, it's only a matter of time. There with our
pole at the prow of the ferry. And here have I built, from these couplets

of metacarpals and metatarsals, a memento, a bone chapel
where the brave may pray and confess and baptize their children.

Self-Portrait with Herbarium

I bought premoistened bathing cloths for invalids
in order to avoid the shared bathroom and shower.
I did not want to eat with the others, so I lived on
saltine crackers I stored in a metal container to keep
away moisture, and wormy apples from the orchard.

I walked the grounds only after dark, and often
ducked beneath the low arbor to visit the graves
of the founders, to thank them for the trees
and meadows, the small gray squirrels and the toads
that leaped in front of me as I walked, and all the plants

that composed my herbarium. I took pleasure less
in the plants themselves than in their categorization.
I went to the library often, but only in the dead
of night. We each had a key, which revealed to me
a degree of trust that seemed, at best, naïve.

Some nights, but rarely, I came upon some other
woman out looking at the moon, which was gold
and swollen. I worried that it would break open
and spill its seed over the meadows.
To me, the animals, deer and foxes and such,

seemed terribly lonely. Even the pond shivered
in its loneliness, and the mountain, for there was
nothing in the landscape to which it could
compare itself. Owls called out to each other
but were only answered by cemeteries.

How did I return to the world? One night,
I walked beyond the stone gate, not through
any intention of escape, but only to seek a rare
flower I could press in the pages of a heavy
book and add to my collection. One quiet

foot in front of the other until I found
myself walking faster, as if pursued,
though no one was invested in calling me
back. Still, I felt like a freed prisoner.
The purple night lifted its heavy curtain

on a day like an unripe peach, orange and softly
green and curved. Mist lifted away
from the fields, revealing that what I'd thought
were boulders were actually cows, reddish,
lifting their white faces to look in my direction.

Self-Portrait with Emily Dickinson (Rebirth of Mourning)

— I lived on that granite edge
— Likened to lichen
— Rain streamed down the fascia
— One pink cypripedium
— Folded like cards or a vulva
— Trillium erectum
— How's that for lonely?
— Crow was cawed out
— Trailed at her hem an unnoticed protégé
— ~~White dress of fog~~
— Pooled in the lower curve of the D like tea in a spoon
— It was the dog that broke her
— Pitcher plant pressed in the herbarium
— If Ginsberg levitated in her attic, I'll eat her Aeolian harp
— Upended a dash to make a headstone
— Weak urine stream
— Vanilla heliotrope lugged through buttercups

Self-Portrait with Sylvia Plath's Braid

Some women make a pilgrimage to visit it
in the Indiana library charged to keep it safe.

I didn't drive to it; I dreamed it, the thick braid
roped over my hands, heavier than lead.

My own hair was long for years.
Then I became obsessed with chopping it off,

and I did, clear up to my ears. If hair is beauty,
then I am no longer beautiful.

Sylvia was beautiful, wasn't she?
And like all of us, didn't she wield her beauty

like a weapon? And then she married
and laid it down, and when she was betrayed

and took it up again, it was a word-weapon,
a poem-sword. In the dream I fasten

her braid to my own hair, at my nape.
I walk outside with it, through the world

of men, swinging it behind me like a tail.

Self-Portrait under Janis's Shoe When She Sang "Ball and Chain" at Monterey Pop, 1967

The sky was gold spangles, the wind a smoker's cough and typhoon. Shade between her shoe-sole and the floor of the stage, a good place to tent-camp, our little fire and pan of Rice-A-Roni. An inch for my boy and me to live in. Like the dark between apples at the fruit stand. Like the inside of a muskellunge. Like what went on under the big belly of the water tower. Like the word "like" coupling the train cars of words so they don't run off on their own down the track of the sentence. If Janis's face was not pitted like the moon, then her face was only pitted, and there was no love to be had. "Like" links the iron ball to the leg iron and love to the whole contraption. Without "like," there is only love or no love to be had. It's like I found my boy in a pile of dirty laundry with a needle in his arm and his lips blue as cornflowers stuck in the middle of Texas. It's like I grabbed his hand and pulled him out of death like a tent worm from its tent in a wild cherry tree. I did find him blue-lipped. I did grab him. Held him like a baby. I held him, my baby. Then Janis stamped her foot and lowered the boom.

Self-Portrait with Freddie M (Invention of Thunder)

I was Freddie Mercury's body. I was the recording studio inside his mouth. His horse teeth were the teeth of my stallion. The show saddle that rubbed my thighs was tooled with scenes of Freddie's early life in Zanzibar. He never fixed his teeth because he didn't want to fuck up his voice. I never fixed my voice because I didn't want to fuck up my teeth. The cow eye I dissected before I learned to be squeamish was his Adam's apple. Freddie's wardrobe was my uncle-by-marriage's fly-by-night mink farm. Freddie's waistcoat painted with pictures of his cats was a cage filled with condemned minks. His cats bred a stillborn black kitten who took up residence between my thighs. Freddie's mustache was my smuggled buffalo. His mustache was my armpit shag. His high note was my low note. His high note set off tornado sirens and wedding bells. Freddie's last thought knocked out my bowling alley. His last T cell apocalypsed my funeral parlor until the embalming table rattled off its runners.

Self-Portrait with Amy (Creation Myth)

That abortion I had in the late '70s grew up to be Amy Winehouse. The music of Richard Hell and the Voidoids fertilized the hell out of my green pear and threatened to turn it into a watermelon. Margaret Sanger herself did the procedure, which involved a bicycle pump and tweezers. By the time "Back to Black" came out, the twin village idiots of my ovaries had already committed themselves to the Island of Misfit Toys from the Rudolph Valentino special we watched every year on the town silent TV on which Mr. Lee had pulled an Elvis the first time he laid eyes on *The Rifleman*. The town blamed all of Mr. Lee's quirks on mustard gas. Yes, Amy was the spitting image of my aesthetic as expressed in my approach to eyeliner I'd invented in 1974 for my theatrical debut as Cleopatra as played by Theda Bara in the silent 1917 film starring Fritz Leiber Sr. as Caesar. All that's left are fragments as the last print burned in a studio fire, so my high school revived it the same year Art Linkletter arrived to give us an anti-drug lecture and I got nicely stoned before giving him a tour of the school's dank hallways and therefore led him down to the creek where he got stung by something due to the insect's attraction to his red sports jacket. I love you, I said to Amy Winehouse the first time I saw the black beehive she'd cooked up for herself. I wrote her a note on a cocktail napkin describing the intersections that led to her conception. That night, I'd kissed the wall over the urinal at CBGB, pee dribbling down my thighs as I'd found my way to the wrong powder room. The moon was starving itself again. Blondie's lips, whether through fate or accident, met mine. A Voidoid spit in my eye. Mikel called sobbing from San Francisco. He'd found a Kaposi's sarcoma lesion on his thigh. This is what made you, Amy. Nothing could kill you, though I tried.

Self-Portrait as Mouthpiece of an Anonymous Benefactor

Flocks of sparrows are waiting to be articulated.
Like Bob Dylan after a concert in the middle
of the night in a strange city, mount your mare
of a motorcycle and ride her into the outer

township, or be Emily, who broke her seclusion
to walk the moonlit fields, only after midnight,
as she was a jazz musician, and only with her
Newfoundland, Carlo. At some point, you must

unpackage your pen. Your hair like an unpeopled
spring-fed pond full of small leeches. Your eyes
like snails on the riverbank where colonial madmen
sailed. At some point, be Arturo at the piano,

land hard on a note like Frank and listen to its echo.
Don't think about things with any degree of largesse.
Be the rock in the pocket that helps the weary poet
sink. There are fawns in the fields: triplets and twins.

Some without lice, without meningitis. I'm giving you
hope like a weird dessert whether you want it or not.
Do you want it? Or not? By the way, the chickens
need to be locked in their box. The fox is hot to trot.

The moon's on a suicide watch. Her swelling
makes her nervous. No, she's not bulimic. It's genetic.
Explore the long sentence. I mean the long prison
sentence. Unmask syntax. So many ways to be a petty

linguist. Government cheese is an aesthetic. Gratitude
for free food is an aesthetic. If you start to smell
like a fish, you've gone too far. The best artists are gutted,
their innards thrown to hungry dogs in a story

by Chekhov. In Chekhov, all the dogs are hungry.
The hairdos are outrageous. There is no such
thing as a personal lubricant. There is spit.
There is something like cement made of tiny

shells and off-brand pearls, flora but no fauna.
I'm not drunk. Are you drunk? This is elementary
and I'm the custodian. I'm who swats the fly
that buzzes when you die. That guy.

Two Floor Mosaics

I – The Unswept Room

"[Sosos] laid at Pergamon what is called the *asarotos oikos* or 'unswept room,' because on the pavement was represented the debris of a meal, and those things which are normally swept away, as if they had been left there, made of small tessera of many colours."—Pliny, *Natural History*

And so here they are, underfoot: nutshells,
stems, pods, a shallot, bones, empty snail shells,
a crooked bird's foot and its shadow.
The mosaicist has even added a mouse,
something alive among the hulls and bones,
sucked clean. Potential energy there.
I imagine a crazy line it might draw if its tail
were dipped in ink, connecting the debris
into something like a constellation, a story.

I imagine also the woman enslaved
to the broom, the one who must
clean up after the rough partiers.
"Crazy folk," I hear her mumble
in her language, sweeping up the real
bones from the ones they call art.

II – Roman Floor Mosaic with the Head of Medusa

"There is a sense of the floor growing transparent and revealing behind it a spatial plunge, like a well . . . and in the moment when the pattern 'reverses' all sense of ground is taken away: the entire surface seems to open down into a void."—Norman Bryson, *Looking at the Overlooked: Four Essays on Still Life Painting*

I use a magnifying glass to see
the image clearly. Yes, the optical
illusion draws me in, but at its bull's-eye

is not a void, but the head of Medusa.
She's looking less terrifying than worried.
The snakes in her hair are doing their

writhing—I almost wrote *writing*.
Her eyebrows are dark and sinuous
as well, rhyming visually with the snakes.

The look on her face is that of a woman
in a predicament: How did I end up
at the vortex of the void? In the depths

of the well of groundlessness
is my face, like the ovary of a flower
but turned to stone.

Passover Lamb

Within the painting's real frame
is a secondary, painted frame composed
of flowers—roses, white lilies, salmon-tinted poppies,
and the blossoms of fruit trees. Inside the floral

frame, she's painted another frame,
this one nearly black, and elliptical, with an angelic head,
as if carved there, and wings, painted at the top. Two clusters
of grapes, one purple, one green, flank the head,

seeming to balance the illusory frame, the grapes so ripe
they appear ready to drop from their stems. Within the false frame's
false window, we see the Passover lamb, prepared for slaughter.
It's painted prone on a black, petal-strewn board,

the legs tied together at the middle joint
so that the pointed hooves fan out from their binding
like the sepal at the base of a bloom. The lamb's curls
are perfectly rendered, as are its flanks,

and soft, folded ear and large, dark eye, cast down.
It fought hard, but the fight is over.
The pink nose rests on the black plane of the board.
I imagine small, huffing breaths, breath that smells sweet

like the breath of an infant. (I remember those days,
when my child's breath was sweet.) All that's left to be finished
is a blade to the throat, a small struggle, a cry,
and then all of those flowers washed in blood.

The painter stages the scene with layers of artifice.
My eye journeys through the floral, the divine, the decorative,
as through theater curtains, until I land upon the lamb
just before—just before the death of tenderness.

What Could Be More Beautiful Than Fede Galizia's Cherries?

On the left, five cherries joined at the stem-end and their nest of nearly black leaves. A small gold butterfly rests its thorax against a leaf. On the right, three pears united, again, at the stem-end. The stems are melded to a bit of the branch of the pear tree that made them. There are dark leaves, for balance with the right, and a single cherry dangles from the elevated tray for equilibrium with the gold butterfly. The profusion of cherries on the silver dish are cherries as we dream of them. Each perfectly spherical, nothing smashed or distorted, no worms or scars, just perfect cherries lit as if each held a small red room, and a girl, and a candle bringing gold up through the red walls. They're sour cherries. Bright red with something yellow in their nature. A tartness that hurts the glands. Did she shine them, wax them? Each is branded by light. And the gold stems waterfall down. She loves them, the chance they give her to paint lines as well as spheres. The stem of the elevated tray is a prototype for "stem." It's engraved with something like valances, curtains behind which Fede, never married, it is written, lies on a small bed in Milan, dying of the plague.

Woman Looking at a Table

Through the grid of the glass windowpanes,
the woman looks in at a table filled with the debris
of a meal. A glass of wine, unfinished. Bread

torn to pieces as if fought over. A cheese in its rind,
a heavy cloud of butter on a plate, half a pear,
and a black-skinned ham, mostly intact,

but enough sliced away to expose the white layer of fat
and the bone, a strange, phallic-looking thing
visually linked to the blade of the knife, which points to it

like an arrow. The woman looks in, hungry-eyed,
her fingers visible on the window ledge.
Her face is odd, sleek like a deer's, with a deer's

archaic smile on her lips. Maybe her mouth is watering,
but I don't think so. I've looked at her gaze
with my magnifying glass, and I think she is looking

at me, coveting my chair. I believe she wants in
to the picture-plane, then through it, to sit where
I'm sitting and to paint the scene as she sees it,

maybe a lone intact pear on a naked table, or the wine
in the glass, to practice rendering transparency.
Maybe she'll turn the ham to hide the gristly bone,

or ignore the ham entirely. Or she'll paint just the grid
of the window with no blue-eyed woman looking in.
Each pane of glass will hold its own measure of the night

and a fingerprint or two. At the bottom of the canvas,
signed with a flourish in the lower right corner,
her name, whatever it might have been.

I Climbed Out of the Painting Called *Paradise*

and padded barefoot across the cold marble floor of the museum.
Outside, down the slate stairway, the ferry to the mainland awaited me.

Awaited all escapees. "Fee!" the Ferrymaster bellowed, but all I had
to offer him was my last apple, a Golden Delicious. He grabbed it

and took a bite with his horse teeth. He was so transparent I could
see the bite as it traveled down his esophagus and came to rest

in the cemetery of his stomach. "Shoes!" he yelled. It turns out
he had a cardboard box full of shoes just for this occasion.

Most escapees were shoeless. I chose a red pair, but they pinched,
so ended up with some worn sandals, the kind that White Jesus

wears in depictions of him walking his lonely road. Once they were
on my feet, the ferry began to glide toward the mainland like a drop

of cream down a small mirror. There was no turning back;
the museum was already lost in memory, which looks like fog.

The Ferrymaster used a long stick, pushed it into the silt at the bottom
of the harbor to guide us along. "That ain't silt," he said, mindreading.

"That's escapees who jumped ship." And I looked into the glassy water
and saw their bodies down there, layers of girls still radiant

with the green-gold light of Paradise, wearing borrowed shoes.
When we reached the mainland, nothing looked familiar, though

it's said we were all born here. The Ferrymaster lowered the rusty
gangplank with a bang. I knew it was rust; the word was nestled

in a cubbyhole in my brain, but I'd never seen it before. "Git!"
he shouted. "And leave the shoes!" He talked always with exclamation

points, which I'd never seen before. They hung over his head
like the droppings of scavenger birds. "What's this place called?" I cried

as he pulled away from the pier, but he only grinned like a skull
grins, without humor. My feet were boiling on the asphalt. I needed shoes,

and coins to buy them with. Shoes and a pile of gold. There were people,
hundreds of them, crisscrossing each other's paths like ants or bees,

carrying tall cups and printed papers and paying me no mind.
Only one, with hair the color of a blood orange, stopped

for a moment, and stared. "Hey, beautiful," he said, which told me
I was real. "Where do I go?" I asked. There were buildings

made of angles that bent sunlight, and roads curving back
on themselves like snakes and crossing each other like crucifixes.

"Home to mommy!" the man said, and he laughed and showed
the gold in his teeth. He was right; I had a mommy. A mother

and a sister. Mother with purple rivers of veins in her hands.
Sister with pale lavender ones at her temples. My mother's hair,

white like a cloud of apple blossoms. I could picture her arranging
peaches in a bowl, and I remembered our house, small and gray,

and beside it a cemetery on a hillside, and I remembered Death,
and how the body is laid inside a box with a pillow for its head

and its hands crossed over its chest, and then the lid is closed
forever and the box is lowered into a vault in the ground,

and the vault receives its lid, and earth is loaded on top of it
and tamped down to keep the body from escaping. I remembered

it all: my yellow room, my little crib with decals of butterflies
and a black-and-white dog and a gold cat on the headboard,

how I'd compose stories about them in my head before I could
speak, and the yellow bird we kept in a cage, and the bog

behind the house, the brown velvet cattails and how they exploded
into sheep's wool in late summer, and the milkweeds, their mysterious

seam like the smile of Mona Lisa with milk on her lips, how they
opened and their seeds were carried on the wind like ships

made of feathers, and Father, wearing a back brace, who would
not be getting well and who could no longer work or play or lift me

into his arms, and I went running toward it, all of it. I wanted
my mother, and this is why I left Paradise.

Notes

Lines in "I Lived My Whole Life in a Painting Called *Paradise*" reference Bruegel's *Landscape with the Fall of Icarus*, William Carlos Williams's poem of the same title, and Jack Gilbert's "Failing and Flying."

"Still Life with Two Dead Peacocks and a Girl" and the other sonnets in that section all represent an invented form. It is fourteen lines, unrhymed, and each line is what Ginsberg called an American Sentence, seventeen syllables straight across the page, without the lineation of haiku. These first appear in Ginsberg's collection *Cosmopolitan Greetings*. "American Still Lifes" and "American Run-On Sentences" are both composed of seventeen-syllable American Sentences.

"The Hand Has Dropped the Fruit and It's Painted Where It Falls" emerges in part from Norman Bryson's discussion of the apparently unplanned nature of Chardin's still lifes in his essay "Rhopography" in *Looking at the Overlooked: Four Essays on Still Life Painting* (1990). ". . . here the form is in a sense ludicrous, or rustic; the hand has simply dropped the fruit where they fall, with the same partial inattention as in reaching for a glass it knows is there."

The last line of "I Look Up from My Book and Out at the World through Reading Glasses" is from the same essay in Bryson's book on still life painting. His discussion of blur in relation to Chardin's still lifes is important to many of the poems in this collection.

In "Two Floor Mosaics" I am indebted once again to Bryson for his discussion of *trompe l'oeil* and "The Unswept Floor" mosaic in "Still Life and 'Feminine' Space," and "Roman Floor Mosaic with the Head of Medusa" in his essay "Xenia" in *Looking at the Overlooked: Four Essays on Still Life Painting*. The epigraphs in this poem are found in these two essays.

Acknowledgments

32 Poems, "Girl in a Picture Frame"

45ᵗʰ Parallel, "Woman Looking at a Table"

A & U Magazine, "Self-Portrait with Double Helix" (under the title "It's Like DNA")

The Academy of American Poets, "Self-Portrait with Sylvia Plath's Braid"

The American Poetry Review, "Self-Portrait with Amy (Creation Myth)" and "Self-Portrait as Mouthpiece of an Anonymous Benefactor"

Ampersand, "Stateline Pastoral" and "Sentences"

Bat City Review, "Self-Portrait with Levitation," "American Run-On Sentences," "I Look Up from My Book and Out at the World through Reading Glasses," "Self-Portrait under Janis's Shoe When She Sang 'Ball and Chain' at Monterey Pop, 1967"

B O D Y, "It Seems at Times that Silence" and "Silence Again"

Crab Creek Review, "Self-Portrait with Emily Dickinson (Rebirth of Mourning)," "Silence Is So Accurate, Rothko Wrote," "The Heroic Penetrates the Quotidian," and "Two Floor Mosaics"

Creative Nonfiction, "Eden: An Outline"

Devil's Lake, "Hindenburg"

Indiana Review, "Walmart Parking Lot"

The Iowa Review, "Still Life with Self Portrait" and "The Hand Has Dropped the Fruit and It's Painted Where It Falls"

Los Angeles Review of Books Quarterly Journal, "Self-Portrait with Freddie M (Invention of Thunder)" and "Memory Fed Me until It Didn't"

Michigan Quarterly Review, "I Look at My Face in a Red Mylar Balloon Tied to a Mailbox," "Bowl," and "Self-Portrait with My Dead Looming behind Me"

The Missouri Review, "There's Some I Just Won't Let Die," "Still Life with Two Dead Peacocks and a Girl," "The Knight's Dream," "Quince, Cabbage, Melon, and Cucumber," "The Last Still Life: The Head of Medusa"

New England Review, "Memento Mori"

The New Yorker, "Still Life with Turkey"

Pank, "Self-Portrait: My Legs"

Quarter After Eight, "I Have Lived My Whole Life in a Painting Called *Paradise*"

The Spectacle, "Self-Portrait with Herbarium"

My gratitude to Hedgebrook, the MacDowell Colony, and Willapa Bay AIR for residencies that supported my work on this book and offered me a glimpse of Eden. Thank you to Jeff Shotts for seeing these poems, and therefore, me. Thank you to Jane Huffman for being my reader, for offering astute critique, and for friendship. Patrick Donnelly: Je t'adore. Love to Gail Wronsky and the badass girls we were. This book would not exist without Conrad Hilberry's lifelong mentoring and friendship, and Gail Griffin's sisterhood, hilarity, and love. Mikel, Kevin: I remember everything about you. My family—mother, father, sister, brother-in-law, nieces: I will always return to you. Dylan—my son, my best reader. I love you.

To the painters and the painted; to the escapees.

DIANE SEUSS is the author of five poetry collections, including *frank: sonnets*, winner of the National Book Critics Circle Award and the PEN/Voelcker Award; *Still Life with Two Dead Peacocks and a Girl*, a finalist for the National Book Critics Circle Award and the Los Angeles Times Book Prize; and *Four-Legged Girl*, a finalist for the Pulitzer Prize. In 2020, she received a Guggenheim Fellowship, and in 2021, she received the John Updike Award from the American Academy of Arts and Letters. She lives in rural Michigan.

The text of *Still Life with Two Dead Peacocks and a Girl*
is set in Adobe Garamond Pro. Book design by Rachel Holscher.
Composition by Bookmobile Design & Digital
Publisher Services, Minneapolis, Minnesota.
Manufactured by Versa Press on acid-free,
30 percent postconsumer wastepaper.